Jj

Bela Davis

Abdo
THE ALPHABET
Kids

abdopublishing.com

Published by Abdo Kids, a division of ABDO, PO Box 398166, Minneapolis, Minnesota 55439.
Copyright © 2017 by Abdo Consulting Group, Inc. International copyrights reserved in all countries.
No part of this book may be reproduced in any form without written permission from the publisher.

Printed in the United States of America, North Mankato, Minnesota.

102016
012017

THIS BOOK CONTAINS
RECYCLED MATERIALS

Photo Credits: Alamy, iStock, Shutterstock

Production Contributors: Teddy Borth, Jennie Forsberg, Grace Hansen

Design Contributors: Christina Doffing, Candice Keimig, Dorothy Toth

Publisher's Cataloging in Publication Data

Names: Davis, Bela, author.

Title: Jj / by Bela Davis.

Description: Minneapolis, Minnesota : Abdo Kids, 2017 | Series: The alphabet |
    Includes bibliographical references and index.

Identifiers: LCCN 2016943890 | ISBN 9781680808865 (lib. bdg.) |
    ISBN 9781680795967 (ebook) | ISBN 9781680796636 (Read-to-me ebook)

Subjects: LCSH: English language--Alphabet--Juvenile literature. | Alphabet
    books--Juvenile literature.

Classification: DDC 421/.1--dc23

LC record available at http://lccn.loc.gov/2016943890

Table of Contents

Jj

Jacob **j**oins his friends.

Jj

Jenna gets jam out of a jar.

Jj

Jade plays jump rope.

Jj

Jim **j**ust turned five in **J**une.

10

11

Jj

Jaime wears jeans in Japan.

Jj

Joe tells a good **j**oke.

Jj

John **j**ogs with his dad.

Jj

Julia enjoys her juice.

Jj

What does **J**osh have?

(**j**elly beans)

More **Jj** Words

jeep

jet

jellyfish

jungle

Glossary

enjoy
to find joy in.

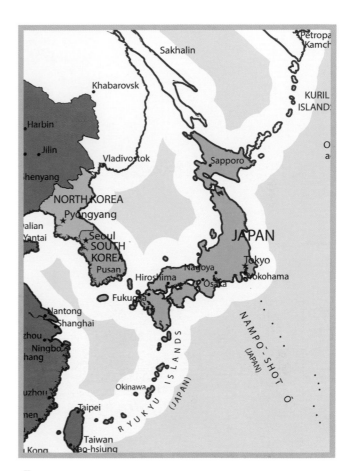

Japan
island country in Asia.

Index

abdokids.com

Use this code to log on to abdokids.com and access crafts, games, videos, and more!